D0886964

$$0°,0°$$

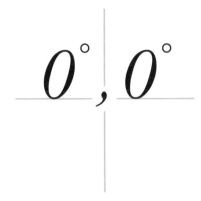

$0°, 0°$

poems

AMIT MAJMUDAR

TRIQUARTERLY BOOKS
NORTHWESTERN UNIVERSITY PRESS
EVANSTON, ILLINOIS

TriQuarterly Books
Northwestern University Press
www.nupress.northwestern.edu

Printed in the United States of America

10   9   8   7   6   5   4   3   2   1

Library of Congress Cataloging-in-Publication Data

Majmudar, Amit.
   0°, 0° : poems / Amit Majmudar.
      p. cm.
   ISBN 978-0-8101-2626-8 (trade paper : alk. paper) — ISBN 978-0-8101-2625-1
(trade cloth : alk. paper)
   I. Title. II. Title: Zero degrees, zero degrees.
PS3613.A3536A613 2009
811'.6—dc22

                                                            2009008617

∞ The paper used in this publication meets the minimum requirements of the
American National Standard for Information Sciences—Permanence of Paper for
Printed Library Materials, ANSI Z39.48-1992.

Contents

Acknowledgments   vii

PART ONE

0°, 0°	5
Mine	6
Answers for the Whirlwind	7
Archimedes Quatrain	11
Subtle Anatomy	12
Michael Reminisces About the War	13
Aggression	15
Instructions to an Artisan	16

PART TWO

The Glassblowers of Venice	19
The Rule	20
M. C. Escher and the Art of Tessellation	21
Satellite Dishes in the Desert	24
Teetotum	25
Merlin	26

PART THREE

The Cherry Blossoms at Walter Reed	31
Wandering Ghazal	37
In Praise of Emergency Evacuations	38

A Pedestrian   39
Texaco Fugue   40
Head of a Bengal Tiger   42
Higher-ups   43
Letter to the Infantry   44

PART FOUR

American Amorobotics, Inc.   51
Matter and Antimatter   52
Moth-eaten   53
Tempest Incantation   54
Distance over Water   55
Static Electricity   56
Ogling Naomi   57
The Disruption   58
By Accident   59

PART FIVE

Riches   63
Wet Nurse   64
Twin Gluttons   65
Patient Histories   66
The Drain   67
Elegy for Professor Liviu Librescu   69
Rites to Allay the Dead   71
The Miscarriage   72

Acknowledgments

The poet would like to thank the publishers of the following publications, in which these poems first appeared:

Antioch Review: "By Accident" (also featured on *Poetry Daily* and anthologized in *The Best American Poetry 2007*)

The Dark Horse: "Aggression" and "Elegy for Professor Liviu Librescu"

FIELD: Contemporary Poetry and Poetics: "Distance over Water" (as "Ghazal: Distance over Water"), "Texaco Fugue," and "Wandering Ghazal" (as "Ghazal: Exile")

First Things: "Archimedes Quatrain" and "0°, 0°"

The Formalist and *150 Contemporary Sonnets:* "The Disruption"

Gulf Coast: "Tempest Incantation"

Image: "Answers for the Whirlwind" and "Michael Reminisces About the War" (also nominated for *Best New Poets 2007* anthology)

JAMA: The Journal of the American Medical Association: "Patient Histories"

Journal of Medical Humanities: "Subtle Anatomy"

Light Quarterly: "Higher-ups" and "In Praise of Emergency Evacuations"

The National Poetry Review: "M. C. Escher and the Art of Tessellation"

New England Review: "The Glassblowers of Venice"

Poetry: "Instructions to an Artisan," "Matter and Antimatter," "Mine" (pseudonymously published; also featured on *Poetry Daily*), "The

Miscarriage," "A Pedestrian" (also recorded as a podcast by Alfred Molina for National Poetry Month), "Riches" (also featured on *Poetry Daily*), "Rites to Allay the Dead," "The Rule" (pseudonymously published), and "Twin Gluttons"

Poetry Northwest: "Wet Nurse"

Salt Hill: "Merlin," "Moth-eaten," and "Satellite Dishes in the Desert" (as "Twenty Satellite Dishes in the Desert")

Smartish Pace: "Head of a Bengal Tiger"

32 Poems: "American Amorobotics, Inc." (also nominated for a Pushcart Prize)

TriQuarterly: "Ogling Naomi" and "Static Electricity"

PART ONE

0°, 0°

      Where equator and prime meridian cross
is the one True Cross, the rood's wood warped and tacked
pole to pole. Constantine's mother wrapped in sackcloth
a splinter of it, Jerusalem souvenir. His fingertips
tickle where they meet in the skies over Fiji.
A nail pegs foot, foot, and Ross Ice Shelf, while the North Sea
baptizes him each time his head lolls. He is convex, racked.
Now the sun hoses him with bleach light, eyes stinging, enough
to make him cough. Now he's spun to face a darkness his
pupils dilate around but can't swallow, not whole. He is
abandoned and loved like clockwork. Meanwhile his dawn-
scouring, dusk-purging blood drizzles to the seafloor,
past leviathan, past shark in a steady drizzle, down
till it spills in the mid-Atlantic's half-scabbed rifts, gashes, its infected
tectonic wounds, fund of land. There, in the heat and smithy,
his blood dyes red the sulfur-loving bacteria
that ask no light, no oxygen, no water of him, that thrive
and sing hosanna with their mouths around the exhaust.

MINE

Pain trains an undisciplined mind.
I will end yours if you end mine.

Little feet, little feet are playing
Hopscotch among the landmines.

Hope has worked miracles before.
If yours couldn't, how can mine?

I could have learned to welcome night,
If only you had been mine.

*How dare you put words in God's mouth,
Amit?* Why not. He put ashes in mine.

ANSWERS FOR THE WHIRLWIND

Has birth ever peeled you apart
Has birth ever hollowed you out
I have seen a woman being transfigured
Into lips her water breaking like the first
Ocean spilling between the thighs of creation
And then between those lips her firstborn crowning
Like a tongue that dips to test the light and scalds
Have you waited in darkness
With nothing but water to breathe
Have you felt pain with anything you've made
Or do you drop these fish-egg worlds black beads
In tidepools of vacuum to hatch for themselves

Do your teeth hurt when you taste sweetness
How about ice have you heard
Ice click against your teeth no what about
The time you let the Arctic drop out of
Your steaming mouth and bob a while and take
Does too much winter make your temples ache
Say do you know what a whip
Feels like no how about a whip of rain
The glaciers do the glaciers you drove north
And corralled in a lattice of locked water
They dream of the freedom to flow once again
The speed and freedom that you took from them
And throw their flanks at the Tropic of Cancer
Like an electric fence and stagger backward
Grasses fossils cities sticking to their soles

Have you dwelt in the house of the not
Yet born and have you paced its floor without
The benefit of footsteps could you handle

Not remembering a thing between creation
And your birthday could you sleep in that
Pitch-perfect dark of not existing yet
And listen and listen unable to add to it
Even the sound of your breathing

Have you stood in the deafening rushes and witnessed migration
On the wing and known from this the cold was coming
Have you hidden your head in a hide not your own
Or shot a creature for its fur and muscle
We've fired the arrows and followed a thread
Of blood out of our hunger's labyrinth
We who had clean hands once and did not need
To wash the fruit we picked or check its skin

Do you feel it down your left arm when your heart
Thirsts for blood and when it thirsts for friendship
Do you feel it in your throat and try to swallow
Does gravity wear on your posture
Does death creep over fields toward you like
The shadow of a white cloud flattening
The grasses it advances over tell me has
Desire ever stripped the stringy husk
Off of your mind and shown you still unripe

If I had been there when you measured out
The earth would you have made it more my size

Do you know how to work with a shovel
Is it graves or foundations you know how to dig
Could you tie me a tourniquet if I required one
How about shoelaces speaking of which
Do you have an idea what it's like to trip
And fall when you do not expect it arms
Shooting out we double over like we've just

Been punched and thump a few steps forth
But we stay on our feet and if there is
A hand that catches us brushes us off
It is not yours

Speak if you have something more than wisdom
Speak if you have sympathy

Would you live with leviathan do you love
Those creatures more who do not stand upright
Were you proud when you filed his teeth
To points so sharp you wouldn't risk a finger
And once you tacked the muscle to his jawbone
Did you grab the still slack snout and open shut
And open shut the maw and think to yourself
Ah this will teach the world what terror is

Do you who know all arts know how to hunger
You may not have that word it has to do
Only in part with the mouth and the stomach
Let me explain it we are little claws
That rake life back and forth like hands in water
Stirring mixing atoms of meat and leaf
Atoms of blood and sap commingling kingdoms
Beast eating plant beast eating beast
Bug eating plant plant eating sun bird eating bug
Beast tipping over in a grunt of risen dust
Bird falling with the small sound camouflaged
Among the raindrops bug snapped in mid-dusk
By the tongue of the twilight
Plant withering stem geyser's spray of leaves
Splashing to earth
So many crisscrossing hungers they darken the soil
Make it fertile make it hungry too for rain
Remodeling desert into wilderness

Who paved roads when they found themselves blocked off
From one another by the wilderness
Who bruised their heels against the wilderness
Who named it tasted every leaf of it at least once
Who remembered which was medicine and which
Was food and which was poison shuffled with
The rest its green no different to the eye
Who sawed and sanded it to crib and casket
And who did that to the wilderness Lord God

With nothing but hands

ARCHIMEDES QUATRAIN

Jerusalem, fulcrum of our uplift,
Is not this rough plank the Cross, laid aslant Golgotha,
The lever with which the philosophers boasted
They could move the world?

SUBTLE ANATOMY

An arm is the spine of an angel wing,
cracked at the elbow. Webbed for gliding once,
we could leap off of cliff or bridge or tower
and saw no problem with a leap of faith.
What happened to it? Ask the suicide.
After the battle in heaven, the good angels,
precursors to the Turks who shamed their captives,
carved and carted off those wings—atrocious—
a mound of wings more chilling than a mound
of skulls: in this case, the contributors
could watch the ground tumor swell. So you see
we have some angel in us, even if
it's the bedeviled kind, stripped of its wings
like a drunk pilot, out of service.

Before Eve met the serpent, she was fleshier
than even Rubens's palette could stomach
and spineless, literally. The serpent
dove in her through the nest-hole anus
until the scorpion-stinger coccyx
slurped in too, and she sheathed him whole.
He straightened her, the breath in a balloon,
into this human posture of rebellion,
this upright and bipedal challenge.
Settled, the serpent sent nerves everywhere,
claiming each inch of her with senses.
Not with an apple but an apple's taste
the serpent ruined her, fossilizing
to the vertebral column. So you see
we have some devil in us too
and dead center at that
commanding everything.

MICHAEL REMINISCES ABOUT THE WAR

. . . They made much of the form
Of their death strokes. You'd think it was tennis, the way
They would ask me for lessons. They stalled,
Though not out of cowardice. Running my obstacle course,
They poked ballet toes through the tires,
Testing the waters of war and declaring them much
Too cold.
        As the battle approached,
They had problems with everything, even the plans
I had drawn. They insisted our troop movements trace
A predictable rose, or at least
Spell EXCELSIOR, LVX, or INVICTVS in bootprints.
Like Lucifer didn't know Latin. Let them
Take the high ground, they sniffed. We fight fair.
A battlefield ought to be level.
             My angels were soft.
They'd been friends with the rebels who marched on them.
Shoulder to shoulder they'd sung in the choir,
Or whatever it is the civilian angels do
During peacetime. It's a miracle we
Won the day. All that talking of theirs,
Those discussions! I listened in once while they sat
Dotting decorative galaxies over their shields.
How can angels, immortal ones, fight to the death?
When the fallen were good, they were deathless; does this
Mean that evil is deathless now, too?
All that thinking does soldiers no good.
Does no good to morale in a camp, in a season for war.
        Somehow we triumphed. The Lord, overjoyed,
Had me wave from the balcony, next to Him. Later,

On the throne with a wineglass, He praised me
For discovering good little killers inside
Of those golden androgynous boys.

AGGRESSION

The whirlwind's come and gone,
spun in place and spun off,
harangued us in what might have been
Hebrew, or might not,

while we held down our hats and ponchos,
reported from the deserted boardwalk,
and bits of roof and compact cars
skipped down the street in somersaults.

Inland, among the chimneys, vanes,
telephone poles, we venture a prow
and pick the occasional stranded kitten
like fruit off a low bough.

Here or there a helicopter,
mistaking us for helpless, clatters down
a rope ladder to starboard
and has to be waved on.

The whirlwind, weakened over
land, humbles the hills, dissolves
in coughs, begins a second sermon,
its vigor halved,

unaccustomed to the give of pines
whose needles, too, know how to bend,
vexed by the flexibility of grass
and the stem's tremendous tolerance.

INSTRUCTIONS TO AN ARTISAN

Into the rood wood, where the grain's current splits
around the stones of its knots, carve eyelashes and eyelids.
Dye the knots, too—indigo, ink-black, vermilion
irises. These will be his eyes, always open, willing
themselves not to close when dust rises or sweat falls,
eyes witnessing, dimly, the eclipse that shawls
the shuddering hill, Jerusalem's naked shoulder.
The body itself? From a wick that still whiffs of smolder,
wax, because wax sloughs a smooth skein on the fingers just
below sensation's threshold. Prop the cross
upright and let the tear-hot wax trickle, slow, clot, taper
into a torso, thighs, calves, feet. Of Gideon Bible paper,
thinner than skin, cut him his scrap of cloth; embed
iron shavings in his forehead,
and, as the wax cools, scrape the rust off an old fuel can
to salt the whole wound that is the man.
Cry, if you feel like crying, and if no one else is there.
Then set it on the counter with your other wares.

PART TWO

THE GLASSBLOWERS OF VENICE

They spin long iron stems, blowing not music
but life into glowing buds, pink growing tips. Silence
swells the glass skin, the most fitting skin imaginable.
At their furnace they forge the orchid's armor,
vases that start in softness cousin to liquid
and end in brittleness no solid acknowledges.
Among glassblowers, inspiration is a matter
of controlled exhaling, as it must be for God
whose whirlwind gentles open the newborn lung,
that first tight birthday balloon, sudden give.
Their job is just as delicate. Stop blowing, stop spinning,
and the bulb droops, crumples, congeals.
Breathe in, and the breath they just gave
burns the wrung brown lung sponge, alveoli
bloodlogged, clusters bright as pomegranate.
The tour of the factory ends in a gift shop,
a garden of tropical chalices, twisting, lurid colors.
One of the old masters within has trapped
his teenage daughter behind the counter.
Indifferent to our marveling, she watches
dubbed sitcoms long off the air back home
and pauses her chewing gum, on occasion,
to blow a bubble of her own.

THE RULE

Discipline. Free will
Doesn't mean freewheel.

But what about Eros? Let
Eros harrow whom he will.

I have sipped my sip
And poisoned the well.

I am well pleased with my thirst.
I know my thirst no evil.

You'll die of thirst, Amit.
If the salt sea wills.

M. C. ESCHER AND THE ART OF TESSELLATION

1

Mathematicians make the toughest audience.
Your complexity has to arabesque a chalkboard
And then, with joyful slashes, above, below,
Cancel itself before their eyes. Simply put,
They expect you to write them a *Paradise Lost*
And then resolve it back to Genesis.

2

It is hard not to wonder if these tricks
Of tessellation might be miracles,
Their way of pleasing both halves of the brain—
Corpus callosum acrackle with cross talk,
Telephone lines athrob beneath the Bosporus—
The most primitive beauty of all, dating back
Before the prime meridian that cleft
Us into hemispheres, east brain and west.

3

Escher, in the Alhambra, learned to take
A Moorish pleasure in repeating tiles.
One seed-crystal of man-made symmetry
Infected a bare wall, self-replicating
Visual virus just short of a soul.
Moors knew that repeating a thing enough times
Can make it true and keep it that way for

At least a couple of centuries. Take
There is no God but God, or the commandment
Banning images: the Alhambra's artists
Defaced their ceiling with no seraphim.
Allah allows no bestiaries. Even Muslim
Mausoleums bear no portraits of their dead,
Mumtāz's image nowhere in the Taj Mahal,
An architectural locket kept empty.
So the frustrated, tightly coiled
Doodling of Allah's born counterfeiters
On the prison-cell walls of iconoclasm
Corroded mosque walls into arabesque grates.
The left-right symmetry of faces, paws,
And wings that they were not allowed to draw
In their kaleidoscopic eyes became
The Regular Division of the Plane.

4

When Escher emerged from the Alhambra, flocks
Interlocked overhead, migrating
In opposite directions, both directions south.
The plane tilted, and the spaces between birds
Turned into fish and populated seas.
The tiles came alive. Taxonomy
Softened their diamonds into feline eyes
Fluorescing with the *Fiat lux*'s flashlight
That stopped him in the Garden. Who goes there?
A goateed Dutchman, with no formal training
In mathematics; a draftsman, showing us
A stage intermediate between matter
And spirit, the sterile Plane seminally split,
Quickened first with symmetry and then with life.

5

His eschatology was reassuring. Death must be
A staircase down to a breezy rooftop, a whole house
Of antigravity staircases where souls
Hurry their millipede legs toward God.
How often he divided the Plane into opposites
Buttressing each other: the bat-winged squat-necked imp
And the Renaissance seraph, the hunchbacked
Eschar-black gargoyle and the upright man
Who circle out of their common plane to shake hands.
The famous hands that draw each other
Answer the hands in the Sistine Chapel.
Between those index fingers, creation
Lightning-bolts all one way, not one salmon
Of imagination thrashing upstream.
Here, one hand is Adam's, one is God's; no one,
Least of all Escher, can say which is which.

6

Nothing's so mystical as symmetry,
Except, I think, the way asymmetry
Can be transfigured into symmetry
By repetition. The kaleidoscope
Is proof that God does not play dice. You can
Make anything sound predetermined just
By rhyming on it twice. Symmetry may
Be pretty, but asymmetry identifies:
The victim's body by a mole, her killer
By his lazy eye.

SATELLITE DISHES IN THE DESERT

They are the flowers Descartes would have invented
if Descartes had taken an interest in flowers.
Cupping their modest portions of the sky
they face any direction but the direction
of our own obvious sun—still heliotropes, only
fascinated by the sun of some other flower's planet.
Every five seconds the satellite dishes
call out in the dubiously universal language
of radio. They are not just mouths
but ears, always more going out
than coming in. Whatever does come
is either static, or a storm
on the sun, or a love letter from life to life
we have failed, again, to translate.

TEETOTUM

A superconductor,
its spin spans
the ineluctable
and chance:

The teetotum,
hybrid of top
and dice, bumps
to a stop,

falling on all
its elbows down
the stairs of its own
shape until

it clatters on
a verdict,
whatever teetotum-
momentum picks,

sage or sot,
kiss or kick,
gyp or jackpot,
one through six.

MERLIN

1. Introduction

Merlin saw the hanging before the crime
and forced down meals before he hungered
and learned to point where lightning would strike
judging from the thunder.

Fire collected smoke to build a hut,
and bums arrived to live in it.
Birds found furnished branches, where they'd sit
on quieting eggs to keep them shut.

2. Merlin at Dachau

A muddy field ruptured.
Jews sprang irregularly,
flowers that they were,
the roots of their necks
sucking up blood
by capillary action
down to the last fleck,
risen rosebuds.
They grew healthy
and donned their rightful clothes
and went home wealthy
to readied ghettoes.

Merlin visited them
centuries later, at the Temple
in Jerusalem.

Histories resolve more justly, Merlin found,
when you study them being rewound.

3. Merlin's Horror

A monstrous queen mother
waited with thighs wide
to be fed her young
by a midwife.

The offering shrieked
as an umbilical cord
tongued forth
and fixed it by the belly.

The mother distended
around her meal like a snake.
She savored it
and took her time

digesting. For nine months
Merlin was horrified.
That used to be a man.
That used to be a man.

4. Merlin Before the Cave Paintings

Now he sits with the first, or for him the last, thinking man
staring up at the original inspiration of mankind
considered from either end in time, the stars.
Merlin knows he will be alone among animals soon.
The thinking man is wondering about the future.

Merlin wants to look in those eyes
incubated with whole cultures
and answer, "What I have seen cannot be changed.
What you try to imagine is part of my memory.
As I pass you, I am coming back from a place
you've started for but will not reach.
I have lived with mankind finish to start,
and I will tell you everything between there and here."

But eye contact between males is a challenge,
and language hasn't been invented yet.

So Merlin shows him how to make crimson paste
and gets him started with the outline of a bull.
The protégé is just old enough
to stay between the lines when coloring.

Outside, Merlin crumples off
his conical comical moon-and-stars hat
and rubs his eyes. "So that was the beginning."
Coming down from the cave's mouth, he braces himself on rocks
like a junkie brailling his bearings on couch edge and coffee table.
How will all he has witnessed
result from that stargazing hunter? Merlin gazes, too,
through the clear spring night and does not understand.
Merlin, too, is only a man.

PART | THREE

THE CHERRY BLOSSOMS AT WALTER REED

1. Invocation

Begin where flesh gives way to phantom pain.

Commence with the canes
tapping coffins down the DC-71's ramp,
the first shots you sing coming from rifles
turned skyward at the march of imperial night,
a volley that scares not one vulture from its hunched
impatient hop and hobble on the tarmac:

Begin not with a breastplate-splitting spear
but pins and needles in a foot that isn't there,
and if in the middle of things
as you're so used to doing, then in the
middle of the hero's leg, or of his twenties,
sing his triumphant march across the mat
from physical therapist to physical therapist
wobbly as a toddler between parents
clapping and encouraging his steps:

Begin with the extubation, with the tilting-up
of the back of the hospital bed,
follow the unwrapping bandage
all six turns around the stump:

Where the treadmill's drone levels off, where
the other sneaker goes to hide, where
the drawer closes on the Purple Heart and the wheelchair
backs away and turns to the door, where
wife lowers warrior into the bathtub
and soaps his thinning hair:

31

Calliope, if you dare,
begin
there.

2. Standing Orders

Bleed if you have to, but turn your wound to the wall.
Declare the police criminals. Train the criminals to use nightsticks.
Stomp your foot and scatter their formations.
Stomp your foot and demand they form an army.

Fire, but not so the microphones pick it up.
Take advantage of this downtime to cry.
Because our hosts disapprove of gambling,
playing cards will be used only to rebuild houses.

Break and enter. Backtrack and superglue.
Kill the mullah, spare the mosque.
Let them try and tip the statue on their own first.
Man this checkpoint, but boy, watch out for those cars.

Get in the Humvee and escort these tankers aslosh
with CAUTION! FLAMMABLE! through the nearest furnace.
Phone calls home are free, but don't let your voice crack.
Return their dignity, but keep their fingerprints on file.

When you get home, be sure to praise your prosthetic legs.
Say you can run faster now. Call them good as new.
Don't mention how you miss the smell of damp socks at dusk.
Get off the bus on your own.

3. Conceived in Love

One whole belly back when she pushes his wheelchair,
she ushers two lives before her own
into maternity stores, Target, the V.A. hospital,

Victoria's Secret . . . Sometimes it happens after his exercises,
after she's bent and straightened his legs
ten times each to keep the blood from clotting,

legs slender and girlish, the hair mysteriously gone.
Keloids thick as railroad ties track up the left calf
where his surgeons dug and found a vein's wisp end

and ripped the root heartward.
They're zero-gravity legs, moon-station legs, ethereal
legs meant to walk on nothingness or water

but never again on the grass. She reaches down,
silk pantie in hand, to stroke
clean the clammy sauna floor of his incontinence.

Sympathetic ganglia, till now in hiding,
return to work, the backup generators
still generative. She takes off her shirt

and leans forward to offer him her breasts
because he still has taste
and he still has hunger.

From a spine's length away, he watches her
as she lowers herself onto an erection
growing out of him like a sapling on the moon.

4. Fit to Serve

Some tried to pump their lungs open with inhalers,
but the track shook them off. Their chests
warbled strange birdsongs at the cold dawn sky.

Far behind them straggled the obese,
every footfall shrugging their bodies lower
until they grounded themselves like dirigibles.

Fresh fog misted up the glasses of the myopic,
who stopped to wipe the plate-glass lenses
walling them off from the finish.

The clubfooted, the found guilty, the senator's son
hobbled, slinked, strutted off the track
and helped themselves to the free Gatorade.

You were still running, though, you and a few others
faintly aware the clamor of a crowd's boots
had quieted and synchronized.

Finish line. Pigeons scattered
at the approach of the judges. Stopwatches dangling,
You boys're the best of them, they beamed. *Heroes.*

Then they had you lower your head
so they could place around your neck, with all
the ceremony of a medal, dog tags.

Meanwhile the ones who had lost the race
watched your glory from safely beyond the fence,
lit each other's cigarettes, and strolled home.

5. The Cherry Blossoms at Walter Reed

Elbows on his knees, in a T-shirt and gym shorts, he waits
under pink explosions of cherry blossom. Their petals
helicopter diagonally as he squints

up at the two men in ties. *Whenever you're ready.*
He picks at the grass and tears a blade
and watches the two halves fall from his fingers.

There's a relaxation to him
that sets him apart from the creased-crisp fatigues
and precisely cocked berets walking the campus.

The discipline, he knows, does not protect you.
Your posture is no talisman, your training's a dry run
at drowning. The suspense has gone

from his shoulders. He has come out
the other side of the mulcher and landed here, a wood chip
under the cherry blossoms at Walter Reed.

Okay. He's ready. His arms rise,
wingspan equaling his height before the tour.
His surgeons kneel under his arms and stand

the way, eight months ago, two of his buddies did
outside Tikrit, where dead bodies under billowing
plastic shrouds gave away the ambush,

the gunner finding out where to swivel
only after the rocket-propelled grenades
had corkscrewed in from both sides,

every vehicle flooring it, but the whole convoy
motionless, dream running . . . *Easy does it.* They tilt him upright
as if he were still on the backboard that buckled him

steady for the airlift west. Then they bow out
like scaffolds tipping away to either side of a shuttle.
Lift off: his arms still wide, what with the high-wire act

walking is. It's only now that my eyes drop
to the complicated bicycle pumps beneath him,
each heel and foot a smoothly curved fiberglass tongue.

This is how tall I was. I remember now.
And he is tall, still proudly muscled, maybe more
muscled from his months in a wheelchair,

arms lunging and retracting, a movable cage, hands
overshooting the rims disdainfully and the spokes invisible,
spinning at threshold, like a ten speed's down a steep hill

when more pedaling adds nothing to the balanced
free fall of your ride . . . *It isn't the same as the treadmill,
is it.* He teeters across the texture of the ground.

No sir. It's better. It's way better.
A wind kicks up, scattering cherry blossoms
across his triumphal march,

and though they steady him more than once,
all I see
is grace.

WANDERING GHAZAL

Measured from Eden, shouldn't every mile of exile
Be thought of as an exile from exile?

I drove through regions known for teas, wines, waters,
But sampled only the varieties of bile in exile.

I tell of distant lands, and in a foreign accent at that.
A boring homebody makes for a beguiling exile.

Each verse is small enough to pack up on short notice.
I was forced to atomize my style in exile.

I have become a doctor of identities,
Refining my photograft and scissorguile in exile.

Flying colorblind, fruit bats in its crow's nest,
A ghost ship colonized this isle with exiles.

Here he is, flying home at last, pretzel crumbs on his shirt,
Porno mag on his lap, bare feet in the aisle: The exile.

Home does not recognize you anymore, Amit,
And declares you the bastard child of exile.

IN PRAISE OF EMERGENCY EVACUATIONS

Rockslides depend on a pebble.
Mudslides creak against a branch.
No one knows the weight of the wedge
of silence chocking an avalanche.

Ripening, ready to fissure,
levees wait for the right storm.
Tanks flank the disputed border.
The hive has yet to form a swarm.

There you are, walking through the valley.
There you are, singing on the snow.
We showed you where sea level was,
but you built your city a mile below,

right smack between the warring tribes.
Omens surround you like nerve gas,
but you just don't heed them, not even
when dead bees litter the grass.

A PEDESTRIAN

He window-shops. He yawns. He checks his watch.
He sips his Starbucks through a spill-proof lid.
No one knows who he is or what he did
Except a black van loitering down the block.
He buys a pack of gum. Briefly he stops
To crouch and read the headlines of the *Times*
Before continuing past 9th and Vine.
His neck prickles. He slows. The coffee drops

& before it has landed he's off like a hound at the races
he is hurdling strollers & ducking a chili dog raised
to the mouth checkered taxis grow fists as he cuts
into oncoming traffic our cellular phones clap shut
in amazement look billowing trench coats give chase
flesh-colored earpieces dangling a flush to their faces

TEXACO FUGUE

The blast crater they were so proud of, Amit,
Hasn't so much as dimpled the empire.

The war had less to do with souls than oil.
Sheikh Shaitan would not let God control the oil.

We feel strong only when the empire's cameras
Record us swearing we will humble the empire.

The devil likes reprocessing temptation:
From wine he made the blood, from coal, the oil.

First they will take our veils, then our faces,
Till we come, over time, to resemble the empire.

Uranium, amphorae, water, bones.
I hope for one thing when I dig a hole: the oil.

From shards of a world much older than theirs,
Children have assembled the empire.

We hold the city, they hold the streets.
In this standoff between shadows, who holds the oil?

They saw your work on the Dome of the Rock
And want you to help them build the empire.

They stole the land, the seeds, the rain, the harvest,
But swear to God they never stole the oil.

The tank and the school are twin symbols of empire.
Is the cause of our squalor as simple as empire?

When the empire comes to burn your village, Amit,
Remember: one of your own sold them the oil.

HEAD OF A BENGAL TIGER

The sahib in his jodhpurs and safari hat
Posed for a portrait with his proud Enfield
And the servants he took with him on the hunt,

Turbaned and mirthless in the Sundarban heat.
It took all six to drag me through the grass
And lay me out like a rug at his feet.

Here I live on, leaping out of the wall
Onto the billiard table's open green,
My teeth forever bared, scaring off time.

His dentures tinkle pinkly in the glass.
He boasts about the man-eater he killed
To a butler who has counted out his pills.

But every night, once he gibbers asleep,
I stir on the wall and I finish my leap
To pace his den on half-remembered paws.

My yellow, candlelight, my black, smoke,
I whisper a tail across his tilted globe,
Still spinning when the morning light shoots through me.

HIGHER-UPS

In khakis with their riding crops,
The English once were hot to trot,
Too chic for the Kikuyu,
Too chichi for the Zulu,
Too hoity-toity for the Hottentot.

Archly they marched in vests of red,
No stains when fuzzy-wuzzy bled.
They set the style, and how:
They look down on us even now,
Festooning fences with their tidy heads.

LETTER TO THE INFANTRY

Wands on the airstrip wave the bombers home—
safe, not a pockmark on a fuselage.
On small, prim wheels they tiptoe to the hangars.

They are done for the day, done for the war.
Their flyboys stroll from air-conditioned cockpits
into an air-conditioned lounge, sunglasses

standard issue out on that open tarmac.
Out in the Gulf, six cigarettes confetti
a carrier's wake as thoughts set course for dinner.

This pixelated green night is yours alone,
yours the heat signatures that hide and hunt it.
Your glove tries the door, your boot kicks it in,

you get a whole half of the road to watch,
you get the clipboard and the sand-trap rifle,
the off-white Fiat that may or may not

be slowing as you raise your hand. Your voice,
repeating *Do not fear,* one of the few
Arabic phrases in your arsenal

along with *Do not move* and *Are you hurt,*
scares women to the walls your shadow darkens.
They shield their eyes against the shard mist rising

from your tank treads. Kneel with a first aid kit
and all they see's the cross. Those "open arms"
that were supposed to garland you instead

cover their heads against you. Children crouch
in a way that reminds you of grade-school drills
back in Ohio, during twister season.

We thought that if we strewed your path with daisy
cutters and bunker busters, you could just
dust off the good guys and ID the bad ones

by teeth fished from the ashes. Fix the plumbing,
hand out some chewing gum, rename a school.
But you showed up, on military time,

to inherit the blame for the rubble, shock and awe
shell-shocked come autumn. Isn't that our pet
pipe dream, to feed this ancient carnivore

money and metal instead of its staple, men?
The origami steel we folded for you,
herons and polyhedrons, throwing stars,

crumple and curl around you, so much litter.
The uplink and the touch screen serve to log
the dead more quickly, and the time of death:

thumb on the stopwatch, radio at the mouth.
A satellite can show you safe zones—dots
of light, throbbing—but satellites can't drive.

You alone carry your hearts to the place
where you must do your killing. You alone
show it the details and challenge it to beat.

I have killed here, but I have not murdered.
I have done violence here but not wrong.
I have done neither God's work nor the devil's.

The taste of the apple still tart on your tongues,
you go home, for a few weeks, to your families.
Same tube, new sitcoms. Pointing at the chest

spared a bullet for the sake of this moment,
you teach your name to your firstborn. Down the street
a tire hangs from a tree. Joy lights the windows

of a trailer the turnpike sighs whishfully past.
Meanwhile, in the cities, we who knew better
than to risk our precious lives like that

sip macchiatos, casually distraught
about an April chillier than usual
and three cents more for a gallon of gas.

I've watched you, just returned. Your posture's more
upright than ours, an evolutionary split.
You're monks observing circuses in late Rome,

crew cuts your tonsures and fatigues your hair shirts—
the unison that answers a drill sergeant,
staccato matins; dawn's run, antiphony.

We immolate you (you, the last ascetics)
to keep the water in the bathhouse warm.
Descending from the mountains, you have found

the Freedom that you preached, in practice, license
shuddering tambourines around the Calf.
Among people who worship their own wills

you alone obey. So many scriptures
exhort us to be instruments, to honor
voices from above us, disembodied voices,

46

the thunder, the whirlwind, the burning bush.
Your commandment speaks itself directly
through plastic that has shaped itself to the ear.

Its voice is human and its motives human.
Forgive our theaters, our mock explosions.
Romantic comedy, action-adventure,

it's all just entertainment or, worse, art
while you are kneeling in the sands and slinging
a whip's exquisite burden on your shoulders.

Sometimes you read your dog tags like they're braille
(the only body armor issued you)
and wonder if the words and numbers stamped there

have sunk as deep as your name will ever sink
in our memories—three-quarters profile,
you know the photo, groomed, ironed, framed

in some ten-second elegy, TVs
shooting their thousand-pixel salute
till our plasma screens, like our hearts and minds,

cut to the sandwich, large Coke, curly fries.

PART | FOUR

AMERICAN AMOROBOTICS, INC.

These days the only way to tell a real woman from a fake one
is to abandon her in a desert and watch what she does.
Real and fake alike will pick some direction to set off in,
eyes leaking water they will later regret wasting.
Each will walk in an unintentional circle until she arrives
at the place where she was abandoned, as if the one
who abandoned her might be waiting there
holding remorseful flowers and checking his watch
against the dinner reservation. The fake woman, though,
will have wandered in a compass-perfect circle
collapsing exactly in the now-blown-over sandprint of her knees,
while the real one will end up a quarter mile
off or pass the spot entirely
because of a curse predating robotics
against our returning anywhere we have left once.
If nothing else the desert reconfigures its dunes,
the embrace having changed in her absence,
harder and colder and even if still warm
warm like a pillow on which a stranger has been dreaming
about sex with a stranger.

MATTER AND ANTIMATTER

When you shake the hand of a stranger
with no shadow, you can never be sure
whether you won't mutually annihilate
like Plath and Hughes at that party in Oxford,
your antimatter counterpart discovered
in the taste of blood from a slit earlobe.
Ascetic or Casanova, monk or mountebank,
everyone has one opposite number composed
in a counterpoint of white noise
that can cancel them out. Monk and ascetic know
how physics can turn the eel-skin whip into a ribbon
and the hair shirt into a Hefner bathrobe.
Neither matter nor antimatter
is wise enough to be terrified from clear
across the room, to dodge the introduction,
down the drink, and cajole the blocking cars
out of the driveway. No, matter sees antimatter
and vice versa. Then, according to an as-yet
poorly understood interaction, each one falls
into the other. Like two black holes *en face,*
emptiness hoping to fulfill itself in emptiness,
like two vacuums mating, matter and antimatter
meet. Soon all that is left of them
are two shattered wineglasses, several biographies,
and a scorched spot on the hardwood floor
where legend has it they danced for the first time.

MOTH-EATEN

The French call them *papillons de nuit*
because they sleep through the day, awaiting
the attainable immolation of candles. Butterflies
of day have wings of stained glass, sheltering
the rose's altar with a cathedral of wing dust.
They open and close like illuminated books, settling.
Butterflies of night replace those rose windows
with the gray of confessional grates, thumbing ash
on the forehead of spring.
                                    One moth
on the wall of my skull, one moth hibernating
the warm hours through, deep in her closet. Moth saliva is slow
acid, a drop of forgetting that eats its weight
in absence. When she exhumes the wedding dress
that fit her before the children,
she will find the tears
already started for her, every moth hole
the size of her bare ring finger.

TEMPEST INCANTATION

This thing of darkness I acknowledge mine,
Black at the pit and black of rind,
A winter-ripe and bitter fruit
That tastes of tar and turpentine,
This thing of darkness, darkest heart,
This sweet gone dark, this heart of mine.
I liked to think myself estranged
From all the lies that worm and wind
And rot it through. I used to cringe
And at its puddled seepage pinch
My nose, that isn't me, that thing
Of darkness is as foul and strange
To me, love, as it is to you.
Done with dissembling, done with shame,
I take it in, I give my name
To crinkled skin that sinks beneath
My thumb, this fruit you picked to eat,
Whose meat you swallowed and whose seeds
You clawed your chest to bury deep,
This poison plum, dark as your bruises,
This thing of *Sorry* and *I swear next time*
And huger ruses,
This fruit whose juice is iodine,
This thing of darkness I acknowledge mine.

DISTANCE OVER WATER

The distance between us is distance over water.
I set out once and have been rowing ever after.

Is this the closest I will come to you, then? Friendship:
The coast no closer though I'm always rowing faster.

I can see the cafés from here, their wine-colored umbrellas.
Over the water I can hear pouring wine, Vespas, laughter.

You preside from your balcony over Provence at play.
Mine is one more craft in the tableau of your afternoon.

Sometimes, when you are telling me about him,
My arms ache with the love I haven't mastered,

And I think of black stones on the beach at Nice
Where footsteps leave no prints and the waves clatter.

I used to live alone on the Isle of Amit. Now I live
Alone between my oars. But I have never been happier.

STATIC ELECTRICITY

Either she is electrically fenced off
at some subatomic level, and this is nature telling me
KEEP OUT, or else the electrons could be flowing
out of me into her, in which case her body bodes well
as a conduit for release. Sometimes I can feel static,
the hair rising along my arm as my fleece crackles
onto the hanger. Static is how unpaired electrons
charge the lowered drawbridge of touch. Each one's impulse
points downwards, each one longs for the unity-
through-dispersal called *grounding*
in physics and in metaphysics called *nirvana,*
the exiled electron repatriated to its profound
fund as the individual becomes at once
paired and anonymous, vulnerable no more
to animal magnetism, no weakness for the opposite charge.
I am still not sure whether that nanovolt
gave me pleasure or pain. Her pen dropped,
I picked it up, and, as my finger brushed her finger,
her skin either stung me with the sound of a kiss
or kissed me with the sensation of a sting.
If all her touches are proportional to that one,
a long-enough embrace may well electrocute
the two of us surging and shuddering at the same time.
Static can build, in bed. Sometimes I fling aside
the covers to get up and write something before
whatever that something is skips from consciousness to dream,
those two worlds touching like God's index finger
and Adam's, poetry passing either way, click.
The blanket throws off tiny white sparks,
as if I were ripping a Band-Aid off an angel.

OGLING NAOMI

"A bowling ball on a mattress" is the metaphor
they use to explain what black holes do to time
and space. Worlds pause,
hesitant as marbles, on the downslope's rim.
The hurricane burr hole in the Milky Way
is a black hole; every galaxy the Hubble can squint
and make out well enough to do a pointillist sketch of
has a black hole for its black pupil, abundant
orange cirrus mere unseeing iris. As for the way
a black hole warps the grid of reality down toward it,
the effect is studied best by observing, on this clear night,
what Naomi does to this room. She may appear
to have a glow, but the light you see is being sucked into her,
barely mapping her image on our retinas before she takes it back
like a hand from the kneeling suitor's lips. And whatever does
cross the event horizon of her gaze
experiences her presence as a crushing sensation.
In death-by-nova, one might yet salvage a blaze of one's own,
but implosion leaves no signature of xenon or debris.
Incompletely understood, her exquisite physics
the sphinx of our speculation, impenetrable (alas), she
is a material ellipsis described best by her anomalous pull
on those who surround her. Her absence draws the ends of sentences
out of our mouths, the glances out of our eyes, even the music
out of these speakers. Crumpling them all as nonchalantly as love letters,
she goes on being the dark center of our mystic swirl.

THE DISRUPTION

I had a world apart before we loved,
Two poles, a compass, and a steady north,
A ground beneath me and a sky above,
No inland dark, no Indies to explore.
I had a universe before we met,
A routine sun, fixed stars, a clockwork moon.
My planets ran the orbits I had set
And played the old Pythagorean tune.

But now you comet chaos love
                              rogue missile
of heat-seeking fire bullet astray
among celestial bodies
                    I fear your kiss will
break my strict night with your naked day
            and from my world's ribs rip a moon and rings
            as your strange tongue teaches my throat to sing

BY ACCIDENT

First she gave me the wound by accident.
Then the tourniquet she tied unwound by accident.

Your friend may want to start running.
I gave his scent to the hounds by accident.

Balloons on the mailbox, ambulance in the driveway.
Bobbing for apples, I drowned by accident.

Did someone tell the devil we were building Eden?
Or did he slither on the grounds by accident?

I said some crazy things, but I swear, officer,
I burned her place down by accident.

Only surfaces interest me.
What depths I sound I sound by accident.

What should we look for in a ghazal, Amit?
Inevitabilities found by accident.

PART | FIVE

RICHES

My mother when she feared that we might starve
Would give us candy taking up her violin
And playing each of us a bar
My mother when we danced the winter from
Our boots and kicked the walls of circumstance
Would write the needed letters over newsprint
And crinkle crackling *fire* till our hands
Came back to us attracted to her gift
My mother painted us a still life and we peeled
And ate the fruit for lunch my mother sculpted
My sister earrings out of pebbles sculpted me
Out of abandonment and earth my mother said
You are not poor until you're at a loss
For worlds you are not rich until like Alexander
You've conquered foreign languages
Somewhere a rich man pokes his fireplace
Reminding it to give him heat she said
Somewhere a rich man's hand lunges in search
Of sweetness down his horn of plenty
But there is not a fruit his fingers recognize

WET NURSE

My father had one brother, who died at two weeks.
Afterwards, my grandmother took his milk
to the children of strangers
and did not go dry. The physiology of the breast
lets it give as long as there is hunger. For years,
if need be, it will gush into any vacuum brought near it,
whether or not the nipple recognizes
the shape of the mouth, whether or not the color
of the breast matches the color of the cheek.
Her next pregnancies flowed into the river
of the lost child's milk. Soon
she thought of it as him giving, not her, him
feeding his newborn sisters, him distributing his unlived life
to every baby she suckled, in each of their lives
claiming one year, the first, the year of innocence,
summing those years into a whole life, and a pure one.

TWIN GLUTTONS

Here's a leg for your gluttony, life: hunched
over the haunch as you are, cramming your masala lamb
and chicken tikka. Meanwhile death fasts in the lotus
position, drinking and pissing, a sieve for Aquafina
aqua vitae and pure Perrier, vintners of Evian
trampling clouds in a vat. This be the pair:
watcher and botcher, scribbler and mercenary,
snapshot hunter facing the crouched Marine
and the crouched Marine facing fire: right brain
watches left brain, moon watches sun, lover
watches beloved from a legally mandated
remove, et cetera watches and so on,
death watches life. Here's viands
for your ravening, life, here's *boeuf bourguignon*
for your *bouche,* mincemeat for your maw:
death will eat later, when he breaks his fast
(the alarm clock sleeps even now at your ear,
life): death will eat later, no steak knife
but a cleaver, no fork but a pitchfork, no spoon
but a shovel, and its appetite will wrap
free will in a shroud of tortilla, entomb ambition
in a pita, and consume all you will and wish
with crematorium hunger. Fire is a stomach:
Death gathers backdraft behind the closed door
of its poker face, death stashes flash and hoards roar
behind chaps clapped shut. You, life, nail boards
of kindle wood over your windows and, panicking,
punch the in case of emergency glass, rip the seal
off what turns out to be a flamethrower. Death,
patiently, burns: any day of the week death could eat you
under the table, life, under the ground.

PATIENT HISTORIES

Some know what ails them inside and out.
They know where they brushed the ivy, and when,
tracing for you around their shins
the border that morning between sock and skin.
After resenting their past doctors by name,
they ask you to spell yours, and write
the letters, as you say them, on a yellow pad.
Medication lists, xeroxed, one for you to keep.
They know exactly at what hour of the night
their pain gave a murmur or turned in its sleep.

But some speak of their ill health haltingly,
the first chest pressure something overheard
across a room packed with more pressing events.
A spouse brings the mole to their attention.
When they first slurred their words is a matter of hearsay;
they have no dates for you, much less a time of day.
And they are always the ones who get
the worst news, whose malignancies have trekked
to lung and liver in the sunshine of benign neglect,
whose backaches turn out to be bone mets, the ones
who felt the lump but figured it would go away.

THE DRAIN

It's like the wobbly,
Clockwise water-

Twister dipping
Softly to the drain—

How the oddly
Gawky mouth

Of a patient dying
Marble-hard, marble-veined,

Warps and draws
With one last breath

His ward, the world,
The sun, his sons

To circle, swim,
Spiral, plunge

Into his singsong-
Gurgle lungs

Down the glugging
Tub drain of his death

Until he sighs it all
Back out, finished

With it. In self-doubt
They tremble there: walls

And windows, skies
And skylines

Slightly diminished,
Subtly dimmed

Minus him.

ELEGY FOR PROFESSOR LIVIU LIBRESCU

Everyone else was startled. Only he turned to the sound
with a nod of familiarity. *Found me here, too.*
Far away wasn't far enough. His chalk clicked on the tin tray.

On the board, the work of his hand:
Diagrams of wings, equations of lift and yaw.
Swift, sure curves, numbers, dashed lines.

The chalk on his fingers was the living white of his hair.
What drew you to the study of aeronautics, Professor?
Things on earth worth escaping:

The column of blue sky between jackboots
leading a boy of twelve into his future
like a column of fire through the desert.

He had heard gunshots before. Not here in Virginia;
in Bucharest, in Tel Aviv. Glass gravel on the pavement.
One backpack bomb could clap the whole sky full of wings.

Brittle as a bird himself, seventy-five years old,
he turned his back to the door, his face
to his students and the bright windows of escape

untouchably far across the room.
I am sorry I could not keep you
innocent of what I know:

That this is what history sounds like up close,
that the flight of bullets has nothing to do
with real flight. Bullets have no wings,

no hearts inside them the way
the smallest sparrows and aircraft do. Bullets
are just shot, and the sky does not love them.

This is what his mother named him: *Liviu.*
As if it were an order, live you live you live.
Live he did, until the shots and shouts

began down the hall, and he recognized
the sound he had escaped all his life.
How fortunate I am to stand here,

to put an old man between you and this.
While his students dropped from the windows
like birds leaving a nest

the door jerked under him five times
with whatever was out there.
Blessing them all with wings,

he bid them *Hurry,* bid them *Fly,*
his eyes lifting from his emptied classroom
to the open windows, and the open sky.

RITES TO ALLAY THE DEAD

It is never enough to close their door.
You have to calm the ripples where they last slept.
The sandals that remember where they stepped
Out of the world must be picked up off the floor,
Their pictures not just folded to face the wood
But slid from the frames and snipped like credit cards.
Open the windows to air out the dark.
Closed blinds attract them, stopped clocks, cooling food.

They'll lick the doorstep like the cat come round,
Remembering you when they remember hunger.
They'll try to billow through their onetime sleeves
And point to your heart as in a lost and found.
The dead will know it, if you love much longer,
And whistle you near through the shuddering leaves.

THE MISCARRIAGE

Some species can crack pavement with their shoots
To get their share of sun some species lay
A purple froth of eggs and leave it there
To sprinkle tidepools with tadpole confetti
Some species though you stomp them in the carpet
Have already stashed away the families
That will inherit every floor at midnight
But others don't go forth and multiply
As boldly male and female peeling the bamboo
Their keepers watching in despair or those
Endangered species numbered individually
And mapped from perch to oblivious perch

For weeks the world it seemed was plagued
With babies forests dwindling into cradles
Rows of women hissing for an obstetrician
Babies no one could feed babies received
By accident like misdirected mail
From God so many babies people hired
Women to hold them babies babies everywhere
But not a one to name When we got home
The local news showed us a mother with
Quintuplets she was suckling them in shifts
A mountain of sheets universally admired
A goddess of fertility her smile
Could persuade the skies to rain Her litter
Slept ointment-eyed in pink wool caps while Dad
Ran his hand through his hair thinking maybe
Of money as he stood surveying his
Crowded living room his wealth of heartbeats

Pizza and pop that night and there unasked inside
The bottlecap was SORRY—TRY AGAIN
You set it down and did not speak of it
The moon flanked by her brood of stars that night
A chaste distracted kiss good night that night
Your body quiet having spilled its secret
Your palms flat on your belly holding holding

Forgive me if I had no words that night
But I was wondering in the silence still
Begetting silence whether to console you
If I consoled you it would make the loss
Your loss and so we laid beside ourselves
A while because I had no words until
Our bodies folded shut our bodies closed
Around hope like a book preserving petals
A book we did not open till the morning when
We found hope dry and brittle but intact

About the Author

Amit Majmudar is a diagnostic radiologist specializing in nuclear medicine. He lives in Columbus, Ohio, with his wife, Ami, and twin sons, Shiv and Savya. His poetry has appeared in *Poetry, First Things, New England Review, Poetry Daily,* and *TriQuarterly,* among other publications, and "By Accident" was selected for *The Best American Poetry 2007.*

green press
INITIATIVE

Northwestern University Press is committed to preserving ancient forests and natural resources. We elected to print this title on 30% post consumer recycled paper, processed chlorine free. As a result, for this printing, we have saved:

1 Tree (40' tall and 6-8" diameter)
654 Gallons of Wastewater
1 Million BTUs of Total Energy
40 Pounds of Solid Waste
136 Pounds of Greenhouse Gases

Northwestern University Press made this paper choice because our printer, Thomson-Shore, Inc., is a member of Green Press Initiative, a nonprofit program dedicated to supporting authors, publishers, and suppliers in their efforts to reduce their use of fiber obtained from endangered forests.

For more information, visit www.greenpressinitiative.org

Environmental impact estimates were made using the Environmental Defense Paper Calculator. For more information visit: www.papercalculator.org.